Boyzone
ON THE ROAD

Boyzone

ON THE ROAD

Rob McGibbon

THE <u>ULTIMATE</u> BOYZONE BOOK

B⊞XTREE

First published in 1996 by Boxtree Limited
Broadwall House, 21 Broadwall, London SE1 9PL

Copyright (text) © 1996 Rob McGibbon
All rights reserved
Photographs supplied by All Action
Designed by Blackjacks, London
Colour reproduction by Scanners

ISBN 0 7522 2252 X

Printed in Great Britain

A CIP catalogue record for this book is available from the British Library.

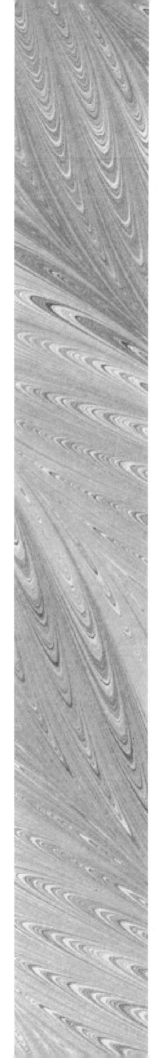

Acknowledgments

I travelled to Dublin in January 1995 to interview all the lads in Boyzone at their homes. By then, they were beginning to experience the early effects of fame, but were concerned about burning out after gaining such instant success. All their fears were unfounded and it has been brilliant to watch them go from strength to strength since then and really crack it. Ronan, Steve, Mikey, Keith and Shane are all likeable, down-to-earth guys, who took a major gamble joining the group and have worked hard for everything they have achieved. I hope this book is a worthy reflection of their work and that there are plenty more chapters to be added in the future. Enormous praise must also go to Louis Walsh, the band's manager, who showed unwavering belief in the boys and has worked tirelessly to get them to the top.

I would like to say a special thanks to Adrian Sington and my editor Clare Hulton at Boxtree for asking me to write this book and for making it such a smooth and enjoyable project. On a personal note, I would like to thank everyone in my family for their constant support in everything. As always, it is greatly appreciated.

The Author

Rob McGibbon began his journalistic career on the Wimbledon News, in South London, and worked as a news reporter and showbusiness writer on several national newspapers before leaving to write books.

In 1990, he co-wrote the first biography of the New Kids on the Block with his father, Robin, also a journalist. They gambled on publishing the book themselves, before the band were famous in Britain, and it became a worldwide bestseller. In the next three years, they wrote biographies of England footballer Paul Gascoigne, TV presenter Phillip Schofield and Simply Red's lead singer Mick Hucknall. In addition, Rob wrote a biography of Take That, which was a bestseller in Germany.

In between writing books, Rob, now 31, is a freelance journalist writing mainly celebrity interviews for newspapers and international magazines. He lives in Chelsea, London. Among his many interests, apart from writing, is soccer and, as a life-long Chelsea fan, one of his proudest sporting moments was playing in a celebrity charity match at Stamford Bridge.

Contents

Introduction

It all began in September 1993, when Irish music agent Louis Walsh hit on the idea of starting his own pop group. He had seen the phenomenal success achieved by New Kids on the Block and their English successors Take That and wondered why a similar all-boy band had never emerged from Ireland.

After placing an advert in a Dublin newspaper, Louis auditioned 300 hopefuls, all dreaming of stardom, before finally finding the five talented and good looking young men he needed. The lucky lads were Ronan Keating, Stephen Gately, Mikey Graham, Keith Duffy and Shane Lynch – they could all sing and dance and had the charisma to become teen idols. The lads were from the Northside of Dublin, and, although they had varying backgrounds, they shared one common interest, a burning ambition to become rich and famous.

For the next six months, they worked tirelessly to mould themselves into Boyzone and, by May 1994, the group was ready to be launched. The next few months would prove to be a dizzy helter-skelter that would change their lives for ever. Their first single, a cover version of the 1980s Detroit Spinners' hit, 'Working My Way Back To You', went straight to No. 3 in the Irish charts and the second release was an even bigger sensation. 'Love Me For A Reason', a cover of an Osmonds record, went to No.1 in Ireland and to No.2 in the UK, selling 600,000 copies. Suddenly, Boyzone was the name on the lips of teenage girls all over Ireland and the UK, and their popularity had spread across Europe.

It had been an incredible beginning, even by the standards of a mad music business where overnight fame is commonplace. But the real Boyzone success story has unfolded since those two early hits. The group could so easily have fizzled out after such a meteoric start, but Boyzone went to work to prove to the world that they are talented and worthy of their fame. The only way they could do that was to pack their suitcases and go on the road . . .

Chapter One

Key to the Future

As the lads in Boyzone celebrated the beginning of 1995, they knew the coming months were critical for them. In their swift and amazing rise to stardom they had scaled heights that other pop groups with years more experience only ever dream of climbing in their entire careers. In less than a year, Boyzone had come from obscurity to have chart success and adulation from thousands of devoted fans. It had been a crazy whirlwind for five lads who, such a short time before, had been part of the anonymous masses in Dublin's Northside. Unfortunately, their rapid ascent had not been welcomed by everyone. It had provoked heavy criticism from many sections of the music media who were dismissing them as worthless bubblegum pop, which would be chewed for a while, then spat out once the sweet flavour of novelty had vanished. As far as the critics were concerned, Boyzone were merely one-dimensional figures only capable of looking good while singing other artists' songs. Sadly, one part of that was true. The group had made its name on the back of hits from previous decades, so more than half the work had already been done for them. But it still hurt Ronan, Steve, Mikey, Keith and Shane to hear so many voices against them

after they had come from nowhere and achieved so much. They wanted to silence those critics and earn their respect. So, as they focussed on the New Year, the lads vowed to prove they were talented, as well as popular.

Boyzone's sprint start had been explosive, but they were acutely aware they could burn out just as quickly. If they wanted to remain successful and last the distance, they would have to slow down and build up their strength. The key to stamina in the music world is quite simple — write your own songs. That is the only sure way to earn the lasting affection of the fans and the critics, as well as the only way to make serious money. There was considerable pressure on Boyzone to quickly follow 'Love Me For A Reason' with another cover version. The record company were convinced that was the best way to secure another hit and underpin the foundations the band had already laid. They felt it didn't matter whose song it was originally and that there was too much at stake to release an original tune from a band without proven ability as songwriters. The argument was basic: why risk failure when the tested formula was so much safer. But the boys saw it differently. They had been irritated and insulted by the sniping about using cover versions to break into the business and felt they were ready to walk without the crutch of other musicians' work. Ronan, Steve and Mikey were emerging as the natural songwriters and had spent many hours during the madness of the previous months writing original songs together for their debut album. They had already completed many and it was clear from those earliest efforts that they had genuine talent. Boyzone recorded some of those songs that January in preparation for the album, which was scheduled to be released later in the year. Also on the track list were several more cover versions, including 'Father and Son' and 'Arms of Mary', but the album would only materialise if their next single was a hit. For that reason alone, it was vital Boyzone got their next move right. If the new release bombed, the album would be put on ice and may never come out. It was a scenario which would see the magical Boyzone flight stall, despite such a spectacular take-off. If that happened, they could easily crash and burn back into obscurity.

Somehow the group had to convince the record company to back their own songs now and not insist on releasing another cover. One of the best songs Ronan, Steve and Mikey had written together was a stirring ballad called 'Key To My Life'. Keith and Shane loved it too, and, as far as Boyzone were concerned, this song was the key to their future. If their own song could be as successful as their cover versions, it would propel them forward with renewed strength. Boyzone had played 'Key To My Life' at a number of gigs and had seen how it moved the audiences. They knew the ballad could be a big hit, and when the record company bosses heard it, they too were quickly convinced of its potential; they were impressed with the lyrics and the melody and felt sure it was as strong as any tune they could dust down from the archives. So, it was decided to take the gamble and make 'Key To My Life' the next single.

The words to 'Key To My Life' are based on crushes Ronan, Steve and Mikey had experienced during their schooldays, particularly on teachers. It was logical, therefore, to make the video to the song in a classroom, and, to add character and atmosphere, it was set in the 1930s with the lads kitted out in heavy wool

Mikey is fighting fit for the tough battle for pop stardom

trousers, waistcoats, collarless shirts and flat caps. The Old Church in the Sandymount district of Dublin was converted into a classroom for the shoot, and the mythical teacher in the lyrics was played by an attractive blonde model, who wielded a cane as the schoolboys looked on adoringly from their desks. Ironically, the make-believe puppy love being filmed inside, was happening for real just yards away. More than 60 or so lovestruck Boyzone fans waited outside the church during the two days of filming. For those girls, the adoration they felt for their idols was as strong as any infatuation Ronan or Steve or Mikey had felt for one of their teachers. That irony would not have been lost on the lads as they ventured out during breaks in filming to sign autographs and pose for photos before having to slip back inside to work.

Jet-setting Boyzone prepare
for departure

The flashback to school life conjured up varying memories for all the boys. Ronan, who was bullied badly, hated school and was suspended once for beating up a bully who had pushed him too far. He said, 'I was never any good at school and was a real messer. Nobody really liked me and I was bullied all the time by a gang of boys. When I was 14, the leader of the bullies mucked me about too much one day and I snapped. I smacked him in the mouth, pushed him into a ditch and hit him a couple more times. The school was very strict about fighting and I was suspended for a week. After the week I had to write a letter apologising and asking to come back to school. The fight worked because the bully never gave me trouble again. He had a bit of respect for me and was really nice after that, but I still hated school and never did my homework. I couldn't wait to leave.'

Steve said, 'Some bad memories came back to me when the teacher in our video held that cane. The teachers at my school had those just in case anyone got out of line. I used to dread going to school, especially when I didn't have my homework done or we had tough exams. The first crush I ever had was on a school teacher. She was 22 and French. I took the class only because she was teaching it. I was about 13 at the time and ended up having to quit French because she drove me crazy. It wasn't difficult for me to play the part in the video because I could easily still be at school, but I was glad when filming ended. I have to admit that my last day at school was probably one of the happiest of my life. Being in a pop band is a lot more fun!'

Although Steve had bad memories of school, Shane looked back fondly on the teacher who captured his heart when he was seven. He said, 'She was a lady called Miss Garland in primary school and I used to think she was the most beautiful person in the whole world. I can still picture her. She had a long brown bob haircut and was really pretty. I also had a crush on my history teacher at The Grange School in Dublin. She had blonde hair and was very feminine. She didn't have much time for men which is probbaly why I liked her. The only problem was, I hated history and ended up failing the exam.'

As the April release date for 'Key To My Life' approached, the jittery nerves began. It was five months since 'Love Me For A Reason' — a long period for any band to be away from the scene. Boyzone couldn't help but fear that the fans would have forgotten them. The pressure was mounting with so much resting on the success of the song. If it was a hit, then the record company would push the button on the next thrilling stage for the group; the release of the debut album would be secured, and the rest of the year would be jam-packed with promotional appearances and trips all over the world, culminating in their first tour of the UK. If the single flopped, everything would be put on hold.

All the fears were unfounded and 'Key To My Life' went to No.1 in Ireland and to No.3 in the UK. The gamble had paid off and had unlocked a dazzling future for Boyzone. They celebrated and breathed a sigh of relief, but there was barely time to savour their success — there was too much work to do. Soon, they were jetting to England to record an appearance for *Top of the Pops* at Elstree Studios, in Hertfordshire. They had last apppeared there to sing 'Love Me For A Reason' in December. Back then, so many fans had waited outside to see them that the BBC security staff had warned Boyzone they would have to provide their own security on future visits. Sure enough, there was a mass of fans awaiting their arrival, and this time Boyzone were prepared and provided the manpower to cope with the crush.

The reception at Elstree was typical of what was in store everywhere Boyzone travelled in an exhausting spring and summer of promotional work across the UK. They made a guest appearance at a fund raising event for childrens' charities in the Midlands and collected £3,000 in a couple of hours by charging £2 per kiss. That's 300 kisses each! They may have had a tiring itinerary, but the lads were happy to enjoy the good sides to fame.

While that may have been fun, there was another gig Boyzone had to perform for a far different section of their fan base — the gay community. A large following had developed among gays since the earliest days of Boyzone, so, as a sign of their appreciation, the band played at G.A.Y.E, London's most notorious club for homosexuals. While their manager Louis Walsh was happy for the band to *sing* for their gay fans, that's where it stopped; he turned down lucrative offers from gay magazines for the boys to strip and declared in the press, 'We value our gay following, but these boys are straight.' So, there were no kisses for the fans after that show!

Despite the adulation from all quarters, none of the group were letting fame go to their heads. Mikey, in particular, remained level headed and remembered all too clearly his days as a car mechanic. That life wasn't so long ago and the deep stains on his hands from engine grease had only recently started to fade. He said, 'Personally, I don't see myself as a pop star. That's what we are called, but I am no different and I have no trouble coasting between my life in Ireland and my life in the group. They are two different worlds, but I'm pretty stable and there is no egomania. I am still the same as before we made any records and I don't think any of us will change. The people who change are generally the ones who believe in their own publicity. We all know that publicity is a smoke screen. We also know that you can be here one minute in this business, and then gone the next. I don't want to sound pessimistic, but we are aware of what may come. Boyzone won't last for ever, but we will enjoy it while we can. Hopefully, it won't happen for a long time, but, if it ends, we will accept it graciously.

'The market was ready for something new and, basically, we have been the only band around. One of the major things that has helped us in the UK is the novelty of being Irish. Almost everyone in Ireland has relatives in England, so the word spread pretty quickly. People seem to love the Irish because we come across as people who like having a good time.

'It sounds strange, but I felt my life has always been heading towards this. I come from a muscial family and I always wanted to make a living out of music, so it didn't come to me as a big surprise. The only thing that has surprised me is how fast it has happened. We were psyching ourselves up for a long slog because it normally takes a lot of bands years to break through, but we seem to have got there in a matter of months — it's unbeliev-able. Our lives are changing every day. I had to give up my job — but there was no crying about that. I get noticed in the streets now and kids come knocking at the door. I was a bit frightened of the fans at first and wondered how it would change my life, but it's not too bad yet. I think the fans in the UK can be more forward, but the kids from my area in Dublin won't go beyond a certain mark, so I think it is a bit easier being a pop star in Ireland than in England.'

Although Mikey's cautious words were wise, Boyzone were, and are, a long way from ending — they were just getting warmed up. They had a continuous flow of public appearances lined up. There was an enthusiastic turn out for their short live gig and signing session at the Virgin Megastore in London's Oxford Street. This was followed by a nerve-racking performance in front of 20,000 at the annual Fleadh Irish festival at Finsbury Park, in North London. Boyzone also got a fantastic response at both the Capital Radio Roadshow and the Radio One Massive Music Tour. At these events, the band proved to thousands in the audience, and to millions listening on radio, that they were a live act to be respected. They showed they were not cardboard cut-outs lip-synching to backing tapes, but energetic performers, with good voices and slick dance routines. Everywhere Boyzone appeared they won the hearts of thousands and earnt cheers from all age groups.

Life on the road was exhausting, but, thankfully, they had reached a level of success where they could enjoy some luxury along the way. In a visit to London the previous year, they didn't have the cash to stay in hotels, so their record company rented them a small flat. They were given £100 to buy food and left to cook and clean for themselves. It was a recipe for disaster for five lads who had never needed to fend for themselves. Predictably, they blew the money on all the wrong provisions – chocolate, biscuits and crisps – and were left to fight over the few morsels of decent food they had bought. By the end of their stay, the flat was a wreck and they were in urgent need of a wholesome meal.

They could now afford to stay in hotels and receive some star treatment, but the memories of that first trip were still fresh in Ronan's mind. He said, 'That was the first time most of us had been away from our parents. We bought far too many biscuits and cakes with our housekeeping money and, by the end, there just wasn't enough food to go round and we were fighting over who had the corn-

Boyzone strut their stuff at the Virgin Megastore

flakes in the morning. But it was the state of the house that eventually got to us. You should have seen what a tip we'd turned it into after just three weeks living there. We never did any housework and I think the washing up only got done twice. There were take-away cartons all over the place, mixed in with smelly socks and clothes everywhere. I was ashamed to invite anyone in. It was a complete dump by the time we moved.'

As the group's diary of engagements continued to build up, it was vital all the lads stayed fit and healthy. Their manager, Louis Walsh, was aware the boys had been wild in their younger days in Dublin, but there was no way any daft behaviour could be tolerated with so much resting on the band. To protect his valuable merchandise, Louis introduced strict contracts which made them legally bound not to do anything likely to risk injury. All the boys are fiercely anti-drugs, but it was still stipulated that they were not to dabble with illegal substances. They were also warned about drinking too much alcohol and banned from taking part in any dangerous contact sports.

One of the incidents which led to such serious discipline was a car accident Shane and Keith had been involved in the previous year. Shane was driving and Keith was in the passenger seat. They were lucky to survive, but Keith still carries the pain of whiplash and back injuries which prevent him from weight training. The crash happened one evening following a group rehearsal, just after they had dropped Ronan off at his house. It was around 1 a.m. and the streets were deserted, so Shane decided to put his foot down in his black Golf GTi. He has always enjoyed driving fast, but he pushed his luck too far that night.

Keith has never forgotten the terror of the crash. He says, 'Once we dropped Ronan off, Shane really put his foot on the floor. He is mad for speed and he really went for it that night – he was driving like a complete maniac. At one point we were doing 110 mph down a narrow street. There was a bend coming up, so Shane

slowed down to about 90 mph, but it was still too fast. The roads were wet and, as we turned, the back wheels slid away and Shane lost control. I knew we weren't going to make it, so I braced myself. I thought we were going to die.

'The car lurched round and then one of the wheels hit the kerb and the car flipped into the air. It bounced over and started rolling. It kept going over for what seemed like ages. I was hanging on for my life.

If we hadn't been wearing seat belts we would have been finished. When the car finally stopped rolling I was left dangling upside down from my safety belt. I knew I was OK, but I was too scared to open my eyes or speak because I couldn't hear a sound from Shane. I felt sure if I looked at him I would see him all broken up and dead.

'I still had my eyes closed when I heard Shane say, "You all right, man?" It was such a relief. I groaned, "Yeah", and then, cool as you like, Shane said, "We might as well get out now" as if he had just parked the car normally, not rolled it over at 90 mph!

'Once we crawled out I was shaking and really nervous. Shane was fine. He had a baseball bat in the boot and he starting hitting the car

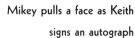

with it and laughing like crazy. I think he is slightly mad, a bit touched. I must admit I started laughing too after a while, but more out of relief than anythng else.

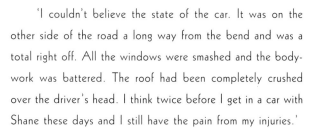

Mikey pulls a face as Keith signs an autograph

'I couldn't believe the state of the car. It was on the other side of the road a long way from the bend and was a total right off. All the windows were smashed and the bodywork was battered. The roof had been completely crushed over the driver's head. I think twice before I get in a car with Shane these days and I still have the pain from my injuries.'

Shane laughs when he recalls the accident. He said, 'I get an amazing rush of adrenalin when I go fast. I love the buzz the fear gives me, but I pushed it too far that night. Thankfully, I always drive with the seat well reclined. If I hadn't been in that position that night, my head would have been taken clean off.

'As I approached the bend I thought we could make it, but the road was a bit wet and there was very little tread on the tyres. I felt the back swing round and then I knew I'd lost it. I just let it happen and wasn't even that frightened. I closed my eyes and heard a few clatters and bangs, but I knew everything would be all right. If Keith and I hadn't walked away from that crash who knows what would have happened to Boyzone.

'We sat by the side of the road and, when the police and fire brigade turned up, they couldn't believe we had escaped with such minor injuries. They started looking in the bushes for bodies because they were convinced someone must have been killed in the smash.

'I was fine and not shaken up at all. If anything, I got a real buzz out of it but Keith was a bit scared. We have had very different upbringings which is why we reacted differently. I used to watch my dad stock car racing when I was a kid and I saw drivers crawl out of the most terrible crashes. Racing cars, speed and crashing has been part of my life.

'For me, crashing is good if no one gets hurt and you don't hit another car. I'd only had the Golf GTi for about four months and it was only worth about £1,500, so it was no great loss. It's not like it was a ten grand car.

'I know Louis wants me to slow down but speed is in my blood. All my friends and I have been mad on cars all our lives. When we were 13 we used to race motorbikes over beaches and golf courses. We were crazy and did jumps over the bunkers and dunes. We fell off loads of times but never got hurt seriously.

'We all got cars as soon as we were 17 and always drive fast. I love the buzz I get from pushing a car to the limit. It's a natural thing for me. I know driving like that is dangerous and people must think I'm a nutter, but I only drive fast at night when the roads are clear and there's no danger of going into other cars. We often race round the small side streets of Dublin or drive round the country lanes at night with our lights off. It is pitch dark and the first person to chicken out and turn their lights on is the coward. It's a daft game but it gets the adrenalin going.

'The only feeling that matches the buzz I get from going fast is when I go on stage in front of thousands of fans. Now that really is something. I guess I'll have to slow down now for the sake of the band and just get my kicks from performing instead. At least that's safer.'

Shane kept to his contract with Louis and eased his foot off the gas, but, while the wild one was tamed, no one could have anticipated that one of the more laid back members of the group, Mikey would get hurt. While filming a video for the album, he fell from a horse. It was not a high-speed fall, but he narrowly escaped horrific injuries when he landed awkwardly on his neck, jarring several vertebrae. A similar accident had left Superman actor Christopher Reeve paralysed from the neck down. Mikey breathed a sigh of relief. He said, 'I'd heard about Christopher Reeve, and when I went down I thought the same fate was for me. I could have been paralysed, so I consider myself very lucky indeed.'

Mikey had a few days rest to get over the intial shock and pain before rejoining the lads on stage for more public appearances. He still had to wear a surgical collar to support his neck, which looked a bit odd during interviews and gigs, but it was a small price to pay for what was a very lucky escape.

Boyzone had slogged through several months of non-stop promotional work across the UK, but their success on the road was suddenly interrupted when distrubing news reached them from Ireland. Rumours had spread that, because the group were spending so much time in England, they preferred English girls to Irish. It emerged that the lies had been started by Take That fans in a vain attempt to create a split among Boyzone followers. It was just childish backbiting from rivals, but Boyzone and their manager took it seriously enough to immediately stop their work in England to return to Ireland for a month-long tour visiting every county. Undeniably, Boyzone would never have made it without their Irish fans, so their loyalties had to be seen to remain with them, no matter what they wanted to achieve away from home. The band were determined that any malicious rumours were quashed before they got out of hand. The record company bosses were not exactly happy with the decision to return to Ireland because they reckoned a month away from the UK represented £1 million in lost revenue. But Louis Walsh was adamant he had made the right move. He said, 'No member of the group has ever said or thought that their English fans are better than their Irish fans. These are scurrilous, evil lies. We love our Irish fans and think they are the best of the lot. We toured every single county and our record chiefs were telling us we were crazy. We could have been making a lot more money out of the country, but our fans at home had to come first.'

Chapter Two
Snap, Cackle and Pop

Take That released their new single at the beginning of July 1995. Inevitably, it went straight to No.1, making it their seventh in two years. It was another remarkable achievement, but, if Boyzone felt slightly envious and daunted by their great rivals' apparent invincibility, the theme of the new release would certainly have eased some of their insecurities. The new Take That song was called 'Never Forget', a rousing tune with reminiscent lyrics of their years of success. Gary Barlow's poignant words reflected on their struggle to the top, but also included the acceptance that, no matter how big they had become, it was all bound to end. Significantly, he wrote. 'Some day soon this will all be someone else's dream', and the chorus repeated 'We're not invincible'. The video to the song was a nostalgic compilation of footage from off-beat moments behind the scenes and the band's on-stage highlights. It was an emotional package, which seemed like an anthem of a group which had accepted that maybe they had reached the summit, and were now focussing on a dignified route down to the foothills.

Boyzone perform at the launch
of their debut album

Although Take That were unbeatable in the charts, the tone of 'Never Forget' gave a clue to the current feelings of Gary Barlow, the driving force behind the band. He was clearly in a reflective mood, so what would that mean for the future of the group? For Boyzone to rise to a higher altitude of popularity, it was essential that there was room at the top. In the teen pop world, there is really only space for one super-group, so Take That would have to be finished if Boyzone were ever to ascend to the summit. The same had been true for Take That several years earlier. They had built up a large

following, but did not make the big breakthrough until their predecessors, New Kids on the Block, had finally faded away. Boyzone knew they would have to be patient, but they certainly got a glimpse of the future without Take That when 'Never Forget' hit the charts.

Although Boyzone respected Take That and everything they had achieved, there wouldn't be too many tears if they did disappear. There had been an undercurrent of animosity for some months and the root of this feeling stemmed from when the two bands met at the *Smash Hits* Poll Winners' Party the previous year. There had been some friction and unfriendliness, but whether it was deliberate on Take That's behalf is not known. The lads from Boyzone were offended and, typically, it was Shane who was more outspoken about that meeting, and less tactful when he considered the possible end of Take That. He said, 'They've got too big for their boots. They've made their money and they're getting lazy and they're not very friendly to us. We can chat to East 17 on a one-to-one level, but Take That seem to

The lads look cool in black for a hot night at Chessington World of Adventures.

Left: Steve has plenty to laugh about

look down on you. I think they are great performers, but I just don't like their personalities.'

Keith added, 'There are a lot of fed up fans who have stopped following Take That because they say they are now out of touch and out of reach. They say Take That don't sign autographs or say Hello anymore. Once they did — now they go to their cars.'

Ronan predicted that Take That's demise would open up the future for Boyzone. He said, 'They have already reached the pinnacle of their success and there is not much further they can go. They've been around for five years and I think they now want out of the teeny-bopper scene. We are younger and hungry for success and we are appealing to the new breed of 12- and 13-year-olds.'

Although Ronan was astute in his analysis of Take That's current situation, there's no way he could have foreseen what was to happen with the Manchester band next. Soon after the release of 'Never Forget', the Fab Five dropped an amazing bombshell: Robbie Williams left. It was a move that left thousands of their fans devastated and one girl in Germany was so distraught she committed suicide. Newspapers and TV stations throughout Britain and Europe set up help lines to counsel those badly affected by his sudden departure. There had been speculation in the newspapers that Robbie had become something of a loose cannon within the Take That camp. He had upset the others by appearing on stage in June at the Glastonbury Festival with Oasis, the drug-taking rebels of pop. He had also been photographed leaving nightclubs in the early hours, drunk and with a variety of girls on his arm.

To be photographed with girlfriends is a cardinal sin for any boy-band member and the others in Take That were not impressed. The new image Robbie was adopting, and the company he was keeping, was in complete contrast to the clean-cut image they had created since the beginning of the group. The full background to Robbie's departure would not emerge for many months, but he did reveal at the time that he had requested to leave after their forthcoming tour because he was sick of the restrictions imposed on him by the management. Once the others knew he wanted out, they let him go immediately.

Robbie was left alone and embittered by the sad end to his time with Take That. The news shocked Ronan more than anyone else in Boyzone. As Robbie had been in Take That, Ronan is the youngest member of Boyzone and is likely to be more vulnerable to the pressures of growing up in the spot-

light. The stress of living his late teenage years in the glare of fame had taken its toll on Robbie and the same was now true of Ronan. He was already feeling the loneliness of being away from home, not to mention the exhaustion of being on the road for months on end, doing a marathon of interviews and public appearances.

Ronan said, 'I was stunned when Rob left Take That. I thought he would be so happy with the group, but the pressures of fame can be so daunting. Already, we're having to deal with the most outrageous offers from our fans. I say a prayer every night and every morning that I won't get into trouble. Many fans attempt to fool our security to get on our tour bus, or try to check into our hotel, or just hang around the foyer waiting for us. It would make you blush to hear the offers of sex we get. Sometimes you feel tempted when you're away from home and there are just four walls of a hotel room to stare at. But we pray that we won't let our families down by falling in with a bad crowd. We also pray that we will stay together, unlike what's now happened to Take That.'

Even with Robbie gone, Take That were still a force for Boyzone to reckon with, and no matter the constant speculation of their future without cheeky Robbie, it was impossible to ignore the stark reality of the vast gulf that separated the two bands. Sure, Boyzone had achieved a fantastic amount since their formation, but Take That were making music history with each No.1 hit. It was obvious that Boyzone had a lot of work to do before they could match the great Take That. One clear example of the different leagues the

groups were in was money. Each member of Take That was already a millionaire and Gary Barlow had amassed an estimated £7 million fortune. Those lads were preparing to buy luxury homes, but, in contrast, Boyzone were, more or less, broke. They had plenty of fame and adulation, but that was not reflected in hard cash. All of them still lived with their parents and were getting by on a basic weekly pocket money scheme from their manager. The figure they received was around £150 per week – a modest sum for a famous pop star. They were expected to live frugally while all the money they had been generating was ploughed back into promoting the band and invested in the next stage of their career. It was not uncommon for Ronan and the others to return to Ireland for a break and have to borrow cash from family or friends to go out. It was an amazing contradiction: they were famous, with hit records behind them and fans staking out their homes, yet they were no better off financially than some of their friends who were working in jobs they had taken after leaving school. They kept going with assurances from Louis Walsh that the

Ronan looks every bit the star with his dark shades and mobile phone and, below, he leads the lads at the album launch gig

money would start flowing in soon. Of course, they believed Louis, but they were annoyed it was taking so long, especially Mikey and Shane, who were used to earning money from working as mechanics. Mikey said, 'We haven't seen much money yet. Things are still being sorted out — and they'd better hurry up!' And Shane added, 'The success of the records has been just brilliant. It is such a high when we do shows alongside East 17 and Take That but we haven't got two pennies to rub together. It makes us laugh when we go home and everyone says we

must be millionaires. We're lucky we have got some clothes sponsorships that put shirts on our backs. We get treated very well. All our food, accommodation and travel are paid for. It's just that we've hardly got a fiver to buy a round of drinks for each other.'

Working hard with no tangible returns was a tough lesson, but the lads always had their minds set on the future. They knew that every drop of sweat now would pay dividends later. They are a shrewd bunch and they were determined from the start not to go the way of so many other pop groups and be ripped off, only to finish their careers rich with fantastic memories, but with empty pockets. They remembered what had happened to Bros, who ended up in debt despite a string of hits. All the lads in Boyzone had taken legal advice before signing to the band, and they were happy that their manager was honest and wanted them to become rich as well as famous, with secure futures whenever their popularity faded.

One vital step to future wealth was writing their own songs. They had proved with 'Key To My Life' that they had genuine songwriting ability. As they were putting the finishing touches to their debut album, Said and Done, they felt proud that seven of the 13 tracks were their originals. They had all played a part in writing at least one song, although the only song credited to them all was the title track, 'When All Is Said and Done'. Not only was it a sense of achievement to write their own material, it was also the only way to secure significant royalties. Shane said, 'We are growing in confidence with writing songs all the time. We are working very hard on making this group the biggest we can. My ultimate dream is to buy a big house on the millionaire belt outside Dublin where the stars live. I was out there recently looking at the flash houses and thought, "Gosh, imagine living right next to where Bono from U2 has his place". I'm just keeping my fingers crossed that in ten years time I might just be able to do it.'

Thankfully, Shane didn't have to wait so many years before he got his first pay cheque from Boyzone. Louis was right — the cash they had been so desperately waiting for finally came through. With the new album in the can, the record company paid a sizeable advance because they were confident of future record sales. It is not known exactly how much money each singer got. It wasn't up in the Take That royalties league, and it certainly wouldn't put Shane straight on to millionaires row, but it was enough for them all to buy cars and put some money in the bank. Shane bought a racy Toyota Corolla, Mikey went for a stylish silver Mazda, Keith got a blue Sierra Cosworth and Ronan went for a sleek black BMW which he planned to customise. Steve had yet to pass his driving test, so he splashed out on one of his main passions — designer clothes. The lads could afford to blow the money because the record company assured them there would be plenty more to follow. Dates had been fixed for their first tour of the UK and they were pleased to hear

ticket sales alone would bring them further revenue, but the big money would flow in from merchandising — the sale of T-shirts, programmes, photos and a whole range of other souvenirs for the fans.

A busy schedule had already built up for the rest of the summer. The release of the album was due in August, which would mean endless TV appearances and press interviews. On top of that, there were jaunts to Europe for extra publicity engagements, and soon the lads would have to begin strenuous rehearsals for their tour in September. The last thing anyone wanted was for one of the boys to have an accident. It had been bad enough when Mikey was injured falling from the horse. But, sure enough, just as everything was set to roll, Shane got hurt.

Despite all the contractural restrictions laid down by the management regarding health and fitness for each lad, no amount of legal paper work could keep an active young man like Shane under control 24 hours a day. Although they were all banned from playing rough contact sports, no one could stop them having a fun knock about in their

Shane smiles through the pain from his broken ankle and, left, he bravely hobbles on stage to cheers from the crowd

spare time, and it was while playing a casual game of basketball that Shane broke his ankle. The ball bounced down a slope and over a small stream. As he jumped across the stream, his left foot buckled and his ankle snapped.

It certainly seems ironic that Shane has walked away from high speed car crashes unscathed, yet was left hobbling in agony after a simple jump. He was rushed to hospital for his foot to be set in plaster and, within a few hours, the pain was subsiding. The headache, however, was just starting to throb in Louis Walsh's head as he considered the almighty problems Shane's injury would cause. The itinerary for the next few months, which had been meticulously planned, was now in jeopardy. Shane is one of Boyzone's more natural dancers, so his energy and rhythm would be sorely missed in the dance routines on stage. They couldn't simply go on without him. But how could he continue on one leg?

The group had insurance cover against any unforseen accidents, so the tour could be cancelled without causing a complete

Boyzone enjoy a free run of the rides at Chessington

financial catastrophe. But the logistics of scrapping a big tour were horrendous. Thousands of fans had to be refunded, but getting their money back would be no compensation for their disappointment. Those fans would suffer and their loyalty to Boyzone could be dented. In the long term, the eventual cost of letting down the fans could prove very costly. Boyzone were still in the embryonic stages of becoming a genuine force in pop music. The key to progression was keeping the momentum. The cyclical whirl of recording, promotion, touring, had to be kept up or they would lose some of the valuable ground they had worked so hard to cover in recent months. It didn't take long for Louis Walsh to realise that there was no alternative but to stick to the original plans and hope Shane could fit in around the others. In the best traditions of showbusiness, the show would go on. Or, in this case, it would hobble on.

Shane missed several public appearances due to his ankle, but he was able to attend the most important function of all – the big launch of the *Said and Done*

The lads cram together for Dragon River and, below, they brace themselves for Rameses' Revenge

album. The record company chose a fitting venue — one of Britain's top amusement parks, Chessington World of Adventures, in Surrey. The lifestyle the five lads had experienced in the past 18 months would easily top even the most exciting white-knuckle ride any theme park could offer. They had lived through dozens of thrills and screams on their crazy rollercoaster ride since breaking into pop music.

It was a beautiful sunny evening for the launch on Monday, 21 August. The boys were greeted at a specially cordoned off section of the park by more than 200 reporters, photographers and TV crews, as well as representatives from their record company and a small group of lucky fans. Also there were other artists, including EYC, Optimystic, Gemini and Sean Maguire, the former *EastEnders* actor who was now making it as a pop star. Looking cool in trendy black outfits and dark glasses, Boyzone gave the select crowd a short live gig inside a marquee. Among the songs they sang were 'Key To My Life' and 'Love Me For A Reason'. Even Shane joined them on stage on his crutches, but he didn't attempt to follow the dance routines. After the gig, there was a big party laid on for the press and the guests. By now the park was closed to the public, so everyone had a free run of the rides. There was plenty of laughter as all the lads from Boyzone, except Shane, squeezed into a log-style boat for the Dragon River ride. At one stage, a TV cameraman sat in front of them to film their reactions as they swirled along the water flumes to the high splash-down drop.

Shane had no excuse to sit out the most terrifying ride at Chessington — Rameses' Revenge, in the Forbidden Kingdom area of the park. All five were nervously pinned into the red seats and secured by hugging shoulders bars. Rameses' Revenge is a giant rotating system which boasts a three-way fear factor — height, speed and water — and spins through 360 degrees at heights of up to 60 feet before lowering the riders over high pessure water fountains. It may have been frightening, but the lads loved it and stayed on for a second spin.

It is every kids' dream to have the free run of an amusement park and it came true for Boyzone and their friends that day. They were laughing and loving every minute of their evening. And all the fun of the pop star fair continued once that magical night was over when their next single, 'So Good', rocketed straight into the charts at No.3. The lads toasted their success, but even that triumph was soon eclipsed when the album went to No.1. It was an incredible achievement. If Rameses' Revenge had been exciting, it paled into insignificance to the exciting ride the lads were enjoying almost every day of their lives. The success of the album was even sweeter because it even brought praise from the critics who had doubted their talent at the beginning of the year.

Shane shows his athleticism
by dancing with his broken ankle
balanced on the crutches

There was hardly any time to catch breath as the next exhilarating peak of the rollercoaster was fast approaching — their first live tour of the UK. It was time to get back to work. Shane was relegated to humble spectator for most of the rehearsal sessions. It was a frustrating time for him. He is not the type to enjoy non-participation. Dancing is one of his passions and, long before Boyzone started, he would dance for hours on end in Dublin nightclubs. But now he had to take it easy and concentrate on getting fit again while he watched the others sweat under the instruction of their choreographer. Even though he could not take part, Shane had to know the intricacies of the show just as well as the others, so he wouldn't get in the way. The last thing the band needed was Shane hobbling around the stage aimlessly. That could easily result in a collision which could aggravate his injury, or get one of the others hurt.

As Shane became more confident on his crutches, he found that he could at least muster up a one-legged dance. He would balance his bad leg over the handles of his crutches so it was suspended off the ground. That left his arms free and he was able to girate his hips and wave his hands maniacally. It was a credit to his athletisim that he could even manage this. It was a funny sight watching Shane dance on crutches, but the lads agreed that, if he was not going to be a skilful factor in the dance routines, he could at least provide some comic relief for the fans. And there was little doubt they would applaud his efforts.

The others worked their way through a gruelling rehearsal period and were finally ready to kick off the tour. Their stylists had selected baggy orange trousers with matching orange cagoule-style jackets and plain white T-shirts for the opening sequence. Sure enough, Shane got the biggest cheer of the night when he hobbled on stage. The girls errupted in screams of approval and roared even louder when he danced on his crutches. The gamble of continuing with Shane had paid off. The first night was a success and there were 20 dates lined up for the rest of September and October, culminating with the last night at the Royal Albert Hall, in London.

When Shane had broken his ankle, the entire Boyzone tour and summer schedule had been thrown into jeopardy and given Louis Walsh an almighty headache. But after the success of 'So Good', a No.1 album and a thrilling start to the tour, the only headache Louis had to nurse was one from too much celebrating.

A cameraman films the boys on Dragon River and, below, Boyzone open their debut tour of the UK

Chapter Three
Secrets, Girls and Fame

The subject of sex and girlfriends became a recurring line of questioning for all the lads during publicity interviews. As their fame grew, so did the focus on their private lives. The management policy — as it has always been with boy bands — was to deny that any of them had girlfriends. Luckily, that was true of Ronan and Shane. Steve, too, was also single after his girlfriend, Joanne, had finished with him when he joined the band because she felt she would never see enough him. Unfortunately, it wasn't true of Keith and Mikey. Both lads had been in serious relationships before Boyzone had formed and they were determined to continue them, despite fears that it would upset the fans should the secrets leak out. Keith was going out with Lisa Smith, an attractive girl he met in 1994 at The POD nightclub in Dublin. Mikey had fallen for another local girl called Sharon Keane. Both boys were told to be discreet and always tell interviewers they were single. The management hoped no one would catch on and they didn't. Well, at least, not for a while.

Mikey's secret would stay safe for a long time, but Keith's was discovered by the press very quickly when he flew off for a week's holiday to Tenerife, in the Canary Islands, off the North coast of Africa. He thought he and his girlfriend and the couple travelling with them would be anonymous on the trip. Details of their itinerary were kept secret, but, unfortunately, he was followed by a sneaky paparazzi photographer once he landed at Tenerife airport. Soon after Keith checked into the five star Parque Santiago Hotel, he headed straight to the pool to sunbathe. As he stretched out on a sunbed, he relaxed

Keith cools off in the pool with his girlfriend, Lisa, unaware they are being photographed

and put all the pressures of fame out of his mind, but, unknown to him, he was still centre stage for at least one pair of eyes.

High on a balcony overlooking the pool, the photographer was hard at work watching Keith's every move. And he couldn't help but smile because laying on sunbeds either side of the singer were two girls – and both were topless. One of the girls was Lisa, the other was her friend. As the camera clicked away, the snapper could see a bumper pay cheque through his telephoto lens. He had one of the heart-throbs of Boyzone, who was meant to be clean-cut and single, in a very embarrassing spread of sexy pictures.

Keith had no idea he had been caught until he was telephoned later at the hotel by a reporter from the *News of the World*. When the reporter said they had pictures of him with the girls, Keith tried to bluff his way out of the situation and denied he knew either of them. Unconvincingly, he said, 'I just met them beside the pool, I don't even know their names. They were just lying beside me. I'm here on my own. Honest, there's no special girl in my life. The girls in the pictures are girls I had just met for the day. Don't get upset, there are no wedding bells or anything like that. I am here on my own, enjoying the super weather. The only other news I have for the fans is that I got a bit sunburnt.'

The excuses seemed rather hollow when Keith's unofficial holiday snaps appeared across two pages in the Irish editions of the *News of the World*. He was pictured playing pool and splashing around in the water with Lisa, but the picture which caused the most embarrassment was him sunbathing between Lisa and her friend. Luckily for Keith and the rest of Boyzone, the damage was limited because the pictures were not published in the main print run of the *News of the World* in the UK. At least his secret was more or less safe from everywhere outside Ireland.

While Mikey and Keith were busy juggling relationships with their teen heart-throb status, the others were trying to cope with the obsessive attention of the fans. Ronan was finding it more difficult than the others. He had never had a serious girlfriend and now it seemed harder than ever to meet someone special. It was an impossible situation: he had thousands of girls in love with him and could easily have a different partner each night of the week, but how would he know who to trust and who were genuine?

At least Mikey and Keith had relationships which were formed before they were famous. Ronan, Shane and Steve would struggle to know if girls were interested in them, or simply their fame and future wealth.

Ronan's love-life was made more complicated because he was still a virgin. He was brought up in a strict Catholic faith which stipulates no sex before marriage. He was more than happy to stick to that rule, but it made meeting a special girl more difficult. In one interview, Ronan talked candidly of his worries. He said, 'I'm only 18 and it's hard being away from home, away from my mum and dad. You can feel so lonely away from your friends and family. I don't have a girlfriend at the moment and sometimes I wish I had someone to rely on, someone to talk to. I often lie awake at night and wonder when I am going to meet the girl of my dreams. I'm a romantic and I'm still waiting for the perfect girl. Believe me, being in a pop band doesn't make it any easier. Relationships are out of the question right now. We are too busy and it just wouldn't be fair on any girl to put up with our hectic lifestyle.

'I tell the fans I am a virgin and they know to look, but not to touch. A one-night stand is not how I plan to lose my virginity. It is a very special thing to me. I come from a good Catholic family and was brought up to respect it. When the girls get fruity, I stand my ground and tell them I have to wait for the special moment when I know it will be right. When it is, I know that girl will be my only sexual partner. Call me idealistic, but I know it's achievable. If you love somebody, anything is possible. Love is the most abused word in the world. It is used and said for the wrong reasons.

'I used to laugh at the kids at school who slept around. They showed no respect by wasting something so important. When I hear about lads coming home from a two week holiday in Majorca, where they put it about, I think it's pathetic. I just wasn't brought up to think like that. Some of my classmates were parents

Spiky haired Ronan, above, sings his heart out while Keith and Steve swing canes in a dance routine during their debut tour

before they finished their GCSEs. That would have scared the life out of me. Keith and his girlfriend have their heads screwed on and they love each other.'

For Shane, the attention from girls was a novelty which he was enjoying. Throughout his teenage years he had been more interested in winning races on his BMX bike, than chasing girls. And, even when he was older, girls always came a poor second to the buzz he got from driving cars fast. Now reckless speed was out of the question, he was starting to enjoy female attention. But, like the others, Shane was only looking for a genuine relationship, not a one-night stand. He said, 'Until recently, I had no time for girls at all – I was only interested in messing about with bikes and cars. Now I get a lot of attention and girls wanting to kiss me, which is fun, but groupies aren't my style. If I had a girlfriend, I'd like someone who'd want me for myself, and not for the pop star they see up on the stage.'

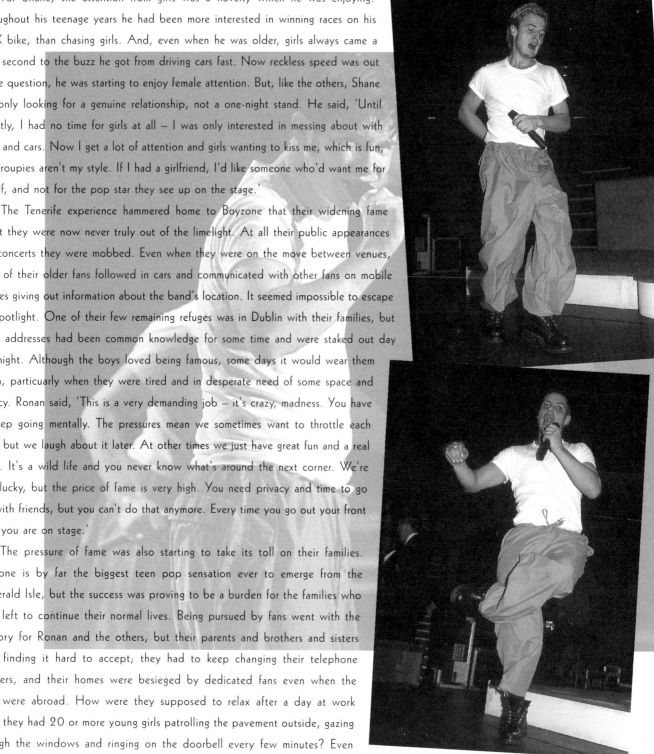

The Tenerife experience hammered home to Boyzone that their widening fame meant they were now never truly out of the limelight. At all their public appearances and concerts they were mobbed. Even when they were on the move between venues, some of their older fans followed in cars and communicated with other fans on mobile phones giving out information about the band's location. It seemed impossible to escape the spotlight. One of their few remaining refuges was in Dublin with their families, but those addresses had been common knowledge for some time and were staked out day and night. Although the boys loved being famous, some days it would wear them down, particuarly when they were tired and in desperate need of some space and privacy. Ronan said, 'This is a very demanding job – it's crazy, madness. You have to keep going mentally. The pressures mean we sometimes want to throttle each other but we laugh about it later. At other times we just have great fun and a real laugh. It's a wild life and you never know what's around the next corner. We're very lucky, but the price of fame is very high. You need privacy and time to go out with friends, but you can't do that anymore. Every time you go out your front door you are on stage.'

The pressure of fame was also starting to take its toll on their families. Boyzone is by far the biggest teen pop sensation ever to emerge from the Emerald Isle, but the success was proving to be a burden for the families who were left to continue their normal lives. Being pursued by fans went with the territory for Ronan and the others, but their parents and brothers and sisters were finding it hard to accept; they had to keep changing their telephone numbers, and their homes were besieged by dedicated fans even when the boys were abroad. How were they supposed to relax after a day at work when they had 20 or more young girls patrolling the pavement outside, gazing through the windows and ringing on the doorbell every few minutes? Even when they were told the boys were away, the fans still insisted on staying. These fans obviously felt happier being near a place directly associated with, say, Ronan or Steve, rather than left staring at posters on their bedroom walls.

There were rare moments when being under siege had its advantages. One day, Steve's mum, Margaret, told fans outside her house that she couldn't talk to them because she had to do the washing up. The girls promptly offered to do it for her — and she accepted!

More often than not, it was inconvenient having fans on the doorstep and the situation worried the boys. Keith said, 'The fans are always knocking on the door saying, "When is Keith coming home?" But this is *our* life and I don't feel our families should have to put up with such behaviour. It happens at all times of the day and they inundate us with phone calls. Even if we change numbers, they manage to find the new ones. Our families get fed up with the hassle.'

Attention from fans and the public in general was now assured wherever Boyzone went, but their popularity also brought a new kind of follower — the merchandising pirates. It hadn't taken long for salesmen to work out that wherever Boyzone went, the fans went, and where there were fans, there was money to be made. The illegal sale of poor quality, rip-off merchandise had first been noticed during the

UK tour. Now, Louis Walsh and the boys were furious to discover that a highly organised underground industry of unofficial Boyzone goods had sprung up and was shadowing their every step. The items that

angered the band most were the second-rate T-shirts and shoddy posters, which were cheap imitations geared to maximise profits, without a thought for giving the fans value for money. But what the bootleggers lacked in quality goods, they made up for in skilled organisation. Thousands of posters and T-shirts were made and sold to gangs which followed the band to every city around the UK. Wherever Boyzone performed a gig, or were booked for a signing session at a record store, the bootleggers lined the routes to the venues and made sure thousands of fans spent their money on the fake goods, not the official merchandise. Boyzone lost in two ways: they missed out on the revenue from selling their own souvenirs and were upset their fans were being ripped off. Louis was angry with the situation. He said, 'Thousands of really bad quaility T-shirts are being put out by the bootleggers.

One wash and they are finished. It has got to the stage where these people are flaunting themselves everywhere we go. They are selling copies of every-thing, including headbands, calendars and key rings. They are taking the money and are certainly not paying us anything. It is costing us a fortune and the lads are really fed up with it. Apart from lost revenue to us, the fans are being sold inferior merchandise.'

Despite the problems with the merchandising pirates, the tour was a fantastic success, with a fantastic last night at the Albert Hall. As the roadies packed up the stage equipment for the last time, the boys headed back to Ireland for a well-earned rest. They only had a few days with their feet up, however, before they were back on the relentless treadmill of promotion. Athough they had a solid fan base in Europe, they had to devote time and effort to keep those foundations firm. So, after all the work in Britain, they headed for the Continent for a whistle-stop promotion tour of Holland, Germany, France, Italy and Spain. They performed for dozens of TV and radio stations, gave countless interviews, and appeared at special signing sessions in each city. Working days on such tours are rarely less than 14 hours, with hardly enough time for a substantial meal or a good night's sleep before they would have to move on to the next city or country. By now, however, the lads in Boyzone were gradually becoming hardened veterans of life on the road.

They returned to Ireland briefly to shoot the video for the next single, their cover version of Cat Stevens' classic, 'Father and Son', and when that was completed, they were off again. This time the destination was the Far East, where, apart from in Thailand, they were virtual unknowns. It was essential they put in some ground work before future releases, so, in a few mad, jet-lagged weeks, the lads crammed in visits to Thailand, Hong Kong, Korea, Singapore and Japan before returning to the UK for the release of 'Father and Son'.

If they had been a little upset by their relative annonymity in the Far East, their confidence was boosted when 'Father and Son', with Ronan on lead vocals, went to No.2 in the UK charts. The success of the single was all the more poignant for Ronan because it was one of the songs he had sung nervously at the auditions for Boyzone 18 months earlier. That day, the song had helped change his life by working its magic on the discerning would-be pop manager who was watching him closely. Now Ronan's emotional rendition of 'Father and Son' was casting its spell over the fans and had given the band yet another hit. Few, if any, of the young Boyzone fans would have heard of Cat Stevens, or his orginal song, but that was

irrelevant. All that mattered was that they loved the group's hit and the boys were pleased to hear that Cat Stevens liked it, too. Boyzone met the singer — now known as Yusuf Islam having converted to Islam — and he praised their cover version.

'Father and Son' stayed in the charts for 14 weeks and, while it was still in the top ten, Boyzone were honoured by having their hands cast in The Wall of Hands at the Rock Circus, in London's Picadilly. The honour ranked them alongside music legends including Michael Jackson, Eric Clapton, Phil Collins and Gloria Estefan. Those honoured have their hands moulded into three-dimensional bronze replicas, which fans can touch when they visit the display. The press photo call was kept secret from fans, but more than 50 found out anyway and were waiting outside before Boyzone arrived. The manager of Rock Circus made an exception and invited the fans in to watch the ceremony from a balcony. Before the plaster had barely dried on the moulds, Boyzone were on the move again with the Smash Hits Roadshow. It was this annual event which had been responsible for making 'Love Me For A Reason' such a huge hit a year earlier. Back then, they had been voted Best Band on the Road and, if there was any section of their fans they had to thank for their success in the UK, it was the *Smash Hits* readers. With that in mind, the band sung their hearts out for them, and their efforts were rewarded, again, when they won the Best Album award and Steve was voted Best Dressed Man of 1995 at the *Smash Hits* Poll Winners' Party.

In the VIP audience that day were the four lads from Take That, who picked up their mandatory bulk of awards to hysterical screams. It had been a tough six months for them since losing Robbie, but they had emerged as strong as ever. However, few people could have guessed what went through Gary Barlow's mind at the party that day. He would reveal a few months later that he had said to himself, 'We cannot be here next year'. Deep down, Gary knew Take That had peaked. They had gone as far as they could and, for him, there was nowhere else for them to go. It would be several months before they would finally break up, but that day, the seeds were sown which would end Take That and leave the future wide open for Boyzone.

Boyzone had one last public appearance in London before returning to Ireland for Christmas. They joined stars and fans for the MTV Christmas Party and entered into the festive spirit by donning Santa hats and singing carols with the youngsters. Even when they were finally back in Dublin, they could not enjoy their own private Christmas until they had done a few more live gigs and TV slots. One of their last appearances that year was on

Boyzone join musical greats in the Rock Circus' Wall of Hands

Gay Byrne's *Late Late Show*. Gay is Ireland's top chat show host and was the man who had given them invaluable exposure a day or so after Boyzone had formed in 1994. On that occasion, they had been raw novices, who barely knew each other. It had been a scary baptism, but on this appearance they were cool and skilful professionals, and Gay was so proud of them that he invited their parents on to the show, too!

At last, Boyzone were allowed to relax and enjoy Christmas with their families. As the festive season went on and the New Year approached, they looked back on an incredible 12 months. They had begun 1995 with many critics writing them off as one-hit wonders, but they had finished the year triumphant with thousands of fans and even the cynics on their side. They had notched up three more top three hits and a No.1 album which had gone platinum. Their first major tour of the UK had been a success and they had jetted across the world to more than a dozen countries. Life as pop stars was most definitely a crazy rollercoaster. Little did Boyzone know, but the magical ride was just getting warmed up.

Santazone – the lads don Father Christmas hats to get in the festive spirit at the MTV seasonal party

Chapter Four
Taking Off and Over

L ouis Walsh told everyone in Boyzone to cherish their few days off over Christmas and New Year. He warned that the short break would be just about their only holiday for the entire year and confidently predicted that 1996 would be even more hectic than the previous 12 months. That seemed hard to believe after everything the five lads had done in 1995, but Louis had his eyes set on a global expansion for the band, as well as bigger tours in Ireland and the UK, not to mention another album. As far as he was concerned, this was just the beginning. From the earliest days of Boyzone, Louis had always aimed for them to reach the heights of success attained by New Kids on the Block and Take That. Now, those targets, which had seemed like blurred visions way off in the distance two years earlier, were now coming into sharp focus. In 1995, Boyzone had sold two million records. Louis's target for 1996 was six million and for the group to perform concerts at major venues across the UK, including several dates at the 12,000 capacity Wembley Arena. He also wanted them to establish themselves in the Far East, Japan and Australia, but, most importantly, Louis wanted them to crack America.

Despite all their hits in the UK and Europe, Take That never really made it in America. They had slogged through several coast-to-coast promotion tours and managed a top ten hit with 'Back For Good', but that was the best they could do. Historically, it has always been incredibly tough for British pop groups to emulate their domestic and international success in the States, where the taste and mood of music fans is impossible to predict. A group can be a sensation in a dozen countries but never even make the charts in America. But, if the magic formula can be found, the rewards are phenomenal. Louis Walsh was convinced Boyzone had a chance to make it in America and he felt that coming from Ireland could work in their favour in a country which so many millions of its citizens have an Irish heritage.

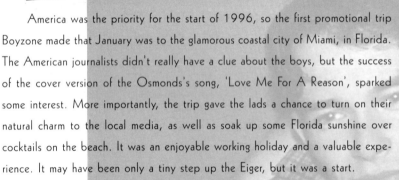

America was the priority for the start of 1996, so the first promotional trip Boyzone made that January was to the glamorous coastal city of Miami, in Florida. The American journalists didn't really have a clue about the boys, but the success of the cover version of the Osmonds's song, 'Love Me For A Reason', sparked some interest. More importantly, the trip gave the lads a chance to turn on their natural charm to the local media, as well as soak up some Florida sunshine over cocktails on the beach. It was an enjoyable working holiday and a valuable experience. It may have been only a tiny step up the Eiger, but it was a start.

Although the whole daunting North American mountain lay before them, the boys were pleased to hear they were already climbing high in the tricky hills of South America. News filtered through that their singles and the album were selling like crazy in all parts of the continent, especially in Brazil. Louis was so pleased that he had the lads take Spanish lessons, so they could issue special releases of their hits in the local lingo in the future. He said, 'The boys are already a huge hit throughout South America and the Spanish lessons are well worth the effort. This is going to be an unreal year – the best ever. They are in the charts in Germany and heading there in France. There's no reason why their popularity shouldn't just keep on growing.'

When Boyzone returned to Ireland, they went straight into the studio to begin remixing the new single and record tracks for their second album. In the meantime, Louis sealed three key commercial deals that would help boost the coffers. He agreed the final design for the Boyzone dolls and signed a major advertising campaign with the makers of Sugar Puffs cereal and one with Cadbury's for their Creme Egg promotion at Easter. The group also got a fantastic buzz when, unexpectedly, they were ranked alongside some of the greats in the music industry by being nominated in the Best International Newcomer category at the prestigious BRIT Awards. Not bad for a band that so many critics had scoffed at.

The new single was an original called 'Coming Home'. The song, which had featured on *Said and Done*, was close to their hearts because it was written when they were homesick for Ireland after long periods on the road. They shot the video in familiar old haunts around Dublin and recruited friends and relatives as extras. But the excitement of releasing the single that February was dulled when the spectre of Take That came back to haunt them. The Manchester band released their new single on the same date. That was annoying enough, but Boyzone accepted it was a genuine coincidence. What rankled them more, however, was Take That's choice of song. They had opted for a cover version of the Bee Gees' 1977 hit, 'How Deep Is Your Love'. This was a song Boyzone had been performing since their earliest gigs in rough Dublin clubs, and they, too, were planning to release it as a single in the future.

It is hard to believe Take That would steal a Boyzone idea, and, sure enough, it emerged later that Gary Barlow had first considered releasing 'How Deep Is Your Love' two years earlier, but had scrapped the idea because he couldn't come up with a suitably different style to the classic Bee Gees' original. The idea was only resurrected when he discovered a slow acoustic approach worked perfectly. Whatever Take That's reasoning, Louis Walsh was fuming. He took great heart in the irony that the mighty market leaders had resorted to a cover version, while Boyzone had released an original, but he still thought his lads had the moral right to the song. He said, 'We have been doing 'How Deep Is Your Love' for two years. It's the very first song we perform at every concert. I am sorry to have to say this, but we

must be blunt about the truth. It is too much of a coincidence that Gary and the lads just happened to pick it as their next single. As far as we are concerned, Take That have nicked our song. We are extremely angry, but what can we do? Unlike Take That, our new single is an original. 'Coming Home' is about the lads in Boyzone being away from home and what they feel like when they come back to their native Dublin. We think it's going to be a smash hit. Boyzone will be very seldom in Ireland this year, so the new release will be particularly appropriate and captures their feelings perfectly.'

Whatever the petty verbal battle with Take That, the Manchester band won the real war — in record sales. They went straight to No.1 and 'Coming Home' went to No.3. Still, it was not a bad effort for Boyzone, who had a fraction of the experience of their rivals, so they were happy with their chart position.

Boyzone had something else to smile about a few weeks later when Take That called an urgent press conference after a story appeared in one of the tabloid newspapers claiming they were about to split up. Gary Barlow, who had inwardly decided the split was inevitable at the *Smash Hits* party, opened the proceedings by confirming the worst to their fans throughout the world. He said, 'Unfortunately, the rumours are true. 'How Deep Is Your Love' is going to be our last single together and the *Greatest Hits* is going to be our last album, and from today . . . there is no more . . .'. The shock news was flashed on television bulletins and the following day's newspapers were filled with obituaries detailing the incredible Take That success story. Telephone help lines were set up to counsel upset fans, just as they had been when Robbie had left the band.

The lads from Boyzone wouldn't have cheered too loudly after the Take That announcement. They are not the types to wallow in what was a sad moment for so many fans and, besides, they had respect for Take That. After all, that band's success had inspired the entire Boyzone dream. The Irish lads had to admit, however, that the news could only benefit them. No matter how well they were doing, they would have always been stuck in the slipstream of the Take That juggernaut. Now it was coming to a complete stop, Boyzone could overtake and move on to an invitingly clear road with nothing in their way.

The prophetic words of Gary Barlow's song, 'Never Forget', had become a reality. Take That's dream now belonged to Boyzone.

The boys didn't have to wait long before they tasted the sort of mania which had surrounded Take That. They flew back to Dublin later in February for a signing session at the main HMV record store to promote the new single. In the previous months, they had been getting a good reception from fans wherever they travelled, but nothing could have prepared them for the shock when they saw the city's main shopping area that Friday afternoon. Grafton Street was in chaos and had been brought to a virtual standstill by more than 6,000 screaming fans. Many had queued overnight to guarantee meeting the boys and some had even travelled from distant parts of England. Extra police had been drafted in to put up crash barriers to allow normal shoppers to move freely and to avoid a stampede when the HMV doors were opened. To say they were like scenes from the height of Beatlemania would be an overstatement, but Boyzonemania certainly arrived in Dublin that day.

There was a long delay while the police and Boyzone's security worked out how to let the signing go ahead without a dangerous crush. Finally, they decided the only way was to monitor strictly the number of fans allowed in the store at any one time. If it wasn't controlled properly, the shop would be wrecked, the boys would be mobbed, and the fans would get hurt. In the end, the fans had to wait patiently as they filed in, a few at a time, to meet their idols. Five hours later, the longest signing session in Boyzone's history, to date, was over. The boys' hands were aching from signing thousands of autographs and their jaws were stiff from constant smiling for photographs. But one man was still beaming – Louis Walsh. He looked at the crowd and said, 'It's terrific to get a welcome like this. Things are really on the up and up. I'm quite confident that we will be the biggest pop group in the UK and Europe within the year. Now that Take That are no more, Boyzone can only get bigger.'

The crazy scenes in Grafton Street must have hit Ronan and Steve a little more than the others; less than two years ago they had worked in shops a short walk from the HMV store. Steve had worked part time for £4 an hour in a clothes shop after leaving school, and Ronan had picked up £3 an hour in a shoe shop on Saturdays. On slow days back then, they had fantasized about fame and fortune as they worked long hours for a modest pay packet. Those dreams were now an amazing reality. The distance from those shops and the HMV store could be measured in metres, but the change from anonymous shop assistants to teen idols was immeasurable.

Louis Walsh had warned Boyzone that their feet would hardly touch the ground in 1996, so, shortly after the Grafton Street hysteria, they weren't surprised to be back at Dublin airport packed for another major journey. It was time to revisit the Far East and Japan to build on the promotion work they had done there the previous autumn. It was a fascinating itinerary, which would incorporate their first trip to Australia, but the fun turned to fear on the Taiwan leg of the tour. International current affairs is hardly the area of research the tour manager of a pop band expects to look into before his band go abroad, but some background on Taiwan would certainly have helped before Boyzone headed for that far off country. They had no idea of the complicated politcal tensions between Taiwan and its hostile neighbour, China. Just as Boyzone were preparing for their visit, China had begun large scale military exercises close to Taiwan's borders.

It had thrown the smaller nation into crisis and the country's army was put on full alert in preparation for an invasion. Boyzone were flying to Taiwan as the tension between the two countries was reaching its peak. Things were so bad that the pilot was ordered in mid-flight not to land because the lives of his passengers could be at risk if the plane was stranded there. It would have been madness to land in a country in such a volatile situation, so the pilot diverted to Bangkok, in Thailand. Thankfully, there was no war between China and Taiwan, but the near miss certainly rattled Boyzone. Ronan said, 'It was very scary and we were pleased that leg of the trip was abandoned.'

The Far East is a culture shock for even the most widely travelled businessmen or tourists, so every day of the trip was an amazing experience for the lads. Although they had made a brief visit to many of the countries before, this time they had longer to soak up the atmosphere and culture of each destination. They were also becoming skilled at coping with draining jet lag by snatching sleep in departure lounges, on planes, and just about anywhere they could. And every day they dosed up on vitamins, supplied by their tour manager, to stop them becoming run down and ill from travelling through so many time zones. The pills, however, couldn't provide a cure for homesickness, which still hit them, and they felt it more than usual when they reached Jakarta, the capital of Indonesia, on 17 March. That is St Patrick's Day for the Irish, but, more importantly for Boyzone fans, it's Steve Gately's birthday! He was 20 that day and, out of the five lads, he was the most homesick. They couldn't help but think of their families back home and how they would all be celebrating like crazy. To cheer themselves and Steve up, they found an Irish bar in the city and toasted both occasions with a good drink up. It was hardly the Northside of Dublin, but it was at least a small taste of home and it would have to do.

Boyzone moved on for the final leg of the tour with their first visit to Australia. They managed to find time to see the traditional tourist attractions, including the Opera House in Sydney Harbour, inbetween a mass of interviews with the media Down Under. They were almost completely unknown there, so it was a case of starting from scratch as they had done in other countries. It was comforting, however, to hear news from home that they hadn't been forgottten; they may have been on the other side of the world, but they were still close in the hearts of their fans and that was proved when tickets for their summer tour of Ireland and the UK went on sale. In mad scenes that were reminiscent of the Grafton Street signing session, more than 30,000 tickets were snapped up within the first few hours of the box offices opening. It was a fantastic response and it made the lads realise there was plenty of work waiting for them once they got back.

Ronan prepares to leave Dublin
for the Far East

Unfortunately, among all the positive signs, there was one piece of bad news which left everyone in Boyzone, and their loyal fans, feeling angry and cheated. By March, more than 1,000 fans had paid £27 to join the newly formed Boyzone fan club. They had given the money in good faith to a company which had been recommended to Boyzone. The fans were expecting a year of exclusive information about Boyzone, but it soon emerged that all was not well with the company. After just one edition, the fan magazine folded and a newspaper discovered that all the money — nearly £30,000 — had already been banked. Many subscribers were demanding their money back, only to be told the company had gone into liquidation. It was an appalling situation for Boyzone. They were furious and embarrassed. Louis Walsh promised immediate action. He said, 'Boyzone are very upset that their fans have been treated in this way. We are determined to find out just what has happened. Everyone who has spent money will be refunded and every subscriber will be invited to come to one of the Boyzone concerts this summer to meet the band.'

Within a few days of discovering the scandal, Boyzone decided to sue the company. The fan club problem would take many months to sort, but Boyzone vowed that the next time they launched their official fan club, they would get it right and do it themselves.

When the group finally returned from their Far Eastern travels, they were given a perfect homecoming. Channel Four's morning show, *The Big Breakfast*, voted them the new Kings of Pop — a crown previously worn by Take That. And, better still, they were honoured at the Irish Music Awards at the Burlington Hotel, in Dublin, with awards for Best Irish Band and Best Irish Single for 'Key to My Life'. They had gambled everything on that song, so it was fitting it should be honoured. Steve smiled as he looked at the trophies and said, 'It's great to get this recognition from people in the industry. It's a terrific boost after being on tour to come home to this.'

Boyzone look the business in Armani suits at the Irsh Music Awards

Chapter Five
Live Across the UK

There was no time to admire their awards, and within a day or so of their glamorous night of triumph, Boyzone were out of the smart Armani suits and back into scruffy T-shirts and shorts ready for some hard graft. The opening of their big tour was only a few weeks away and there wasn't much time to prepare for what would be a highly pressurised and draining schedule.

They locked themselves away in the dance studio and sweated for up to nine hours a day perfecting dance routines and stage directions. It was a period of intense work. Boyzone pride themselves on slick, synchronised routines and they were striving for even higher standards for this tour, with faster and more complicated steps. Learning the moves involved exhausting

Above, Ronan sings for the fans and, left, Boyzone dazzle them with silver jackets for the opening of the new tour

physcial exercise and extreme mental patience. They are all perfectionists who expect nothing but the best from each other. None of the lads were prepared to put up with second best, so tension would be at its worst when one of them slacked or was slow getting a routine exactly right. The work they put in now, behind closed doors, would show in the performance they gave in front of thousands. This would be their biggest tour to date and would see them play in venues with an average audience of more than 5,000, so there was no room for short cuts.

Inbetween the physical exertion of the dancing, they also had to fully rehearse all the songs with a drummer and a keyboard wizard, who would provide all the music. On top of working with the musicians, Boyzone had to agree on a stage design. It had to be visually eye-catching, yet simple enough for the roadies to dismantle quickly for overnight transportation to the next destination. The lads also had to be fitted for the several costume changes that would occur during each concert. It was soon apparent that doing a full-scale tour was a complicated and tiring business — long before a single note was sung. If the pressure at work wasn't enough, there were even more serious matters for Keith and Mikey to consider in their private lives. As they rehearsed for the tour, they were keeping big secrets from the fans — they were about to become dads!

Fatherhood is not the role you would expect two rising teen heart-throbs to adopt and was hardly an ideal development for the band. Louis Walsh and the three other lads would have known for months about the impending new arrivals, but they must have been in shock for quite a while after first hearing the news. The babies would be arriving at a critical period for the group. The tour was imminent and that would be followed by a further blitz on the charts, with new singles and the second album in September. It was a time when they would all have to stick together and work solidly. How could Keith and Mikey do two such demanding jobs? Surely, it was impossible to be a dad and a pop star.

Thankfully, any worries were eased when the two lads pledged their commit-ment to Boyzone. They realised they couldn't walk away from all the work and progress the band had made in the past two years. It would shatter the dreams of too many people behind the scenes, not to mention Ronan, Steve and Shane, and

thousands of their loyal followers. A compromise was worked out and it was decided that Keith and Mikey would keep to the same routine as the others, but they would be given time to be with their girlfriends and babies as soon as the slightest gap in the schedule appeared. It was a logical solution. Keith and Mikey were happy in the knowledge that, although they would miss valuable time with their children now, the work they were doing would provide secure futures for their families.

The main concern now was how the fans would react to the band becoming something of a Babyzone. It was Keith's secret which was discovered first. The newspapers confirmed that the woman expecting his child was shop assistant Lisa Smith — the girl with Keith in the sneaky pictures in Tenerife. It emerged they were now living together in a £90,000 Dublin home, which Keith had bought with his Boyzone earnings. It must have come as a shock to the fans. Up until then, Keith had denied even having a girlfriend, let alone being involved to the extent where he had settled down and was about to be a dad. Keith would not have enjoyed living a lie for so long, but he'd had no choice after strict orders were laid down by his managers to keep the relationship secret. Thankfully, as far as anyone could tell, there was no backlash from the fans. If anything, they were happy for him, even if some were slightly envious of Lisa. Mikey's secret would be revealed in the press a few weeks later, but the fans were reassured to learn that parenthood would not affect Boyzone. The babies would stay firmly in the background.

Keith finally spoke about the prospect of becoming a dad. He said, 'I'm really thrilled about everything that is happening in my life. I love my fans, but myself and Lisa are happy, too. People now know we are together and I plan to stay with her. It has been great to share a house and I am looking forward to our future together. I'm so excited about the baby, I can't think about anything else. Lisa and the little one are the most important things in my life and I want to protect them. I am public property, but Lisa isn't, so I want to look after her and keep her out of the limelight. It's been quite a stressful time, but she needs to take things easy right now and I don't want her to get upset. I don't mind if the baby is a boy or a girl, so long as it is happy and healthy. Becoming a dad for the first time is a big thing in a man's life and it is the first grandchild for both our mums, so they are looking forward to it, too.'

He didn't have long to wait following that interview. A few days later, on Monday 22 April, Lisa was rushed to Dublin's Rotunda Hospital at 6 a.m. She was in labour for many hours, but finally gave birth to a healthy baby boy weighing 8 lb 7 oz, who they called Jordan after Keith's American basketball hero, Michael Jordan. Keith was due to travel to Europe that day for a promotional appointment with Boyzone, but he pulled out at the last minute to be with Lisa and Jordan. Sadly for Keith, though, he could only be with them for a few days before he had to leave to be on stage with his other family, Boyzone. He said, 'It has been hard work preparing for this tour and keeping my family happy. But now we're going out on the road, I'm determined to enjoy it and make the most of it.'

The exertion is etched on Steve's face as he performs a solo spot

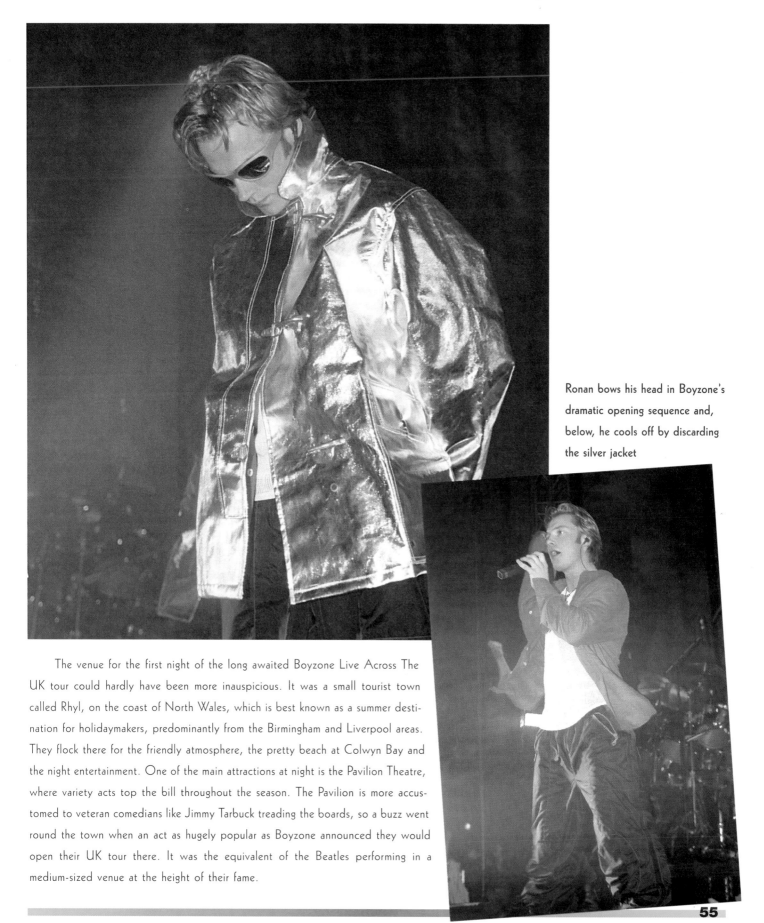

Ronan bows his head in Boyzone's dramatic opening sequence and, below, he cools off by discarding the silver jacket

The venue for the first night of the long awaited Boyzone Live Across The UK tour could hardly have been more inauspicious. It was a small tourist town called Rhyl, on the coast of North Wales, which is best known as a summer destination for holidaymakers, predominantly from the Birmingham and Liverpool areas. They flock there for the friendly atmosphere, the pretty beach at Colwyn Bay and the night entertainment. One of the main attractions at night is the Pavilion Theatre, where variety acts top the bill throughout the season. The Pavilion is more accustomed to veteran comedians like Jimmy Tarbuck treading the boards, so a buzz went round the town when an act as hugely popular as Boyzone announced they would open their UK tour there. It was the equivalent of the Beatles performing in a medium-sized venue at the height of their fame.

Pauline Cerefice, who works in the box office at the theatre, remembers when the tickets went on sale. She said, 'We have never seen anything like it at the theatre or in Rhyl before. People were queuing up the night before the tickets went on sale. They were mainly parents getting tickets for their children, but there were a few older girls as well. There was a real air of excitement about the town. We couldn't believe such a big group would play here. We normally have much older variety acts, so Boyzone was quite an event. It was fantastic for the kids, a real treat.'

The young girls among Rhyl's 25,000 population had one man to thank for the unexpected arrival of Boyzone — Louis Parker. Louis was brought up in Rhyl and, conveniently, he is Boyzone's tour agent and the man responsible for the tour venues. If it was not for Louis, and his deep affection for the town, there is no way the group would have played a theatre as small, or as out of the way, as the Pavilion, which only has a 1,030 capacity. For this tour, Boyzone were aiming for venues with a minumum of 4,000, working up to 12,000 for Wembley Arena.

Whatever the Pavilion lacked in size, it easily made up for in atmosphere. When Boyzone opened their tour there on Monday 29 April, the quiet little theatre was transformed by a noise level worthy of twice the number in the audience. Pauline Cerefice took a look inside soon after the first support act started and was amazed at what she saw. Normally, the seats are filled with adults sitting respectfully, but this night was completely different. She said, 'I have never seen the theatre like it. All the girls were up on their feet dancing right from the very start of the support acts. And they stayed standing and dancing until the end of Boyzone's performance. It was a brilliant atmosphere. They were screaming and shouting and singing — they loved every minute.'

Keith gives pop fame the thumbs up

The two nights at the Pavilion were a perfect start for Boyzone. They were a suitable warm-up, and gave them the chance to try out their new routines, without the added pressure of a much bigger audience. The reception they got from the lucky few at Rhyl was tremendous and it boosted their confidence for the nerve-racking schedule that lay ahead.

Just after the opening two nights in Wales, Mikey was suffering nerves of a different kind — those of an expectant father. He had to rush back to Ireland where his girlfriend, Sharon, was close to having their baby. His worries were soon eased when she gave birth to a healthy 6 lb 10 oz girl. Sadly, Mikey only had a day with his daughter, Hannah, before he had to fly back to England to be on stage at the Ipswich Regent, in East Anglia, on 2 May.

Split into two main legs, the tour would take Boyzone a total of nine weeks to perform 50 concerts at 35 different venues. They would play in Dublin and Belfast and several concerts in Scotland and Wales, but the bulk of the gigs would be in every major town and city across the length and breadth of England. A one-off gig at the Langelands Festival in Denmark was thrown in for good measure. The first leg of the tour began in earnest after the Ipswich concert. From there, Boyzone travelled constantly for a month, clocking up thousands of miles as they and their roadies weaved their way up and down and across the UK. The first destination was the North West, where they performed in Liverpool, Manchester, Blackpool and Blackburn. Then they returned south to play the Apollo, in West London, before moving on to Wolverhampton, in the Midlands, and Bristol in the West Country. It was a haphazard, illogical route, but the key factor was that each venue was a sell-out and Boyzone were a smash hit in every town. Their performances were getting rave reviews in all the provincial newspapers, and one national tabloid pop column declared after the London gig, 'Catch Boyzone on this tour and get set for the latest teen sensation.'

Personal security became a priority on the tour. The five lads were the irreplaceable elements of the entire operation. Equipment, transport, even crew members who fall ill, can be replaced, but the five teen idols were precious cargo which had to be protected at all costs. This is why highly trained bodyguards were hired for the tour. They earnt their money soon after Boyzone hit the road when the group received death threats. It was never revealed who was the target, or if there was a genuine danger, but a sinsiter letter was sent to a Dublin evening newspaper stating that one of the boys would die during the tour. The letter was postmarked from Galway, a pretty town on the west coast of Ireland. Police were called in to investigate the threat and the tour minders were put on alert. Louis Walsh said at the time, 'It probably comes from a crank, but no one can ever be certain about these things.'

Despite that one example of hatred, the only danger Boyzone really faced on the tour was too much adulation. The reception from the fans was amazing and the boys were beginning to lap up the attention and the thrill of big concerts. Ronan said, 'We love the excitement of live shows and the buzz we get from the fans. It sends a shiver up my spine when I hear their screams. It means a lot to us to think that they care so much. It's also fairly good fun fending off the girls and trying to keep our clothes on when 50 girls want to pull them off. It certainly helps us to stay fit!'

Keith added, 'The buzz I get from performing live is the best part of being in the band. At first, I thought I was only in it for the money, but now I just love the thrill of a concert.'

Steve also loved performing, but was finding it tough to cope with the emotional extremes of life on the road. By nature, he is incredibly shy and will always be the quietest in any normal social gathering. But his character changes the moment he walks into the beam of the stage lights. He is transformed from quiet, sensitive Stephen Gately from Seville Place, to super-confident Steve, the entertainer and principle heart-throb of Boyzone. The adrenalin and excitement carry him through all the shows, but he found himself retreating into his protective shell almost as soon as the lights had dimmed. The draining yo-yo of emotions was creating confusions and he was finding it hard to deal with two such contrasting sides. On one level he was the centre of attraction to thousands of screaming fans, and on the other he was alone in his hotel room, or cutting himself away from the others during the long hours on the tour bus travelling to the next town.

In one candid interview Steve talked of his lonelines and insecurities. He said, 'People say I look good, but, to be honest, it makes me cringe. I don't think I have the best face and, more often than not, I blush to the roots if I think a girl fancies me. I worry all the time. I fret over my complexion, if my hair is OK, whether my clothes fit, or even what I should say to people. I've seen down more clevages than I've had hot dinners and girls come up to me and say saucy things. But I'm just a shy guy who would prefer to get to know them first. Sometimes I get so lonely I have to wipe the tears away. I miss my home, my family — even my teddy bears! I can end up missing my mum so much that I find myself having a cry in my hotel bedroom. But I know that's something I will have to learn to live with.

'The area I am from is not posh, but it was my home before Boyzone and will remain my home as long as my family live there. All day and most of the night a gang of fans wait outside my house for me. When I come home, I usually stop for a chat and sign autographs. They are so sweet to wait for such a long time to see me but, once inside, it is my time. That is when I really unwind. I know I will always have my own little bedroom and the 200 teddy bears I have collected over the years.

Steve is a star on stage but he is shy away from the spotlight

'Mum is always there for me when I land back in Dublin after touring the world. Of course, I dream that one day I shall have my own family and a special girl in my life to settle down with, but, for the moment, I'll have to be content to snuggle up to my teddies. Winnie the Pooh might not be the most passionate play-

mate, but at least I am saving myself for Miss Right, whenever she chooses to walk into my life. Until then, I will always be a mummy's boy — and proud of it!'

Thankfully, Steve and the others were learning to cope with the weird and wonderful world of touring. By the time they reached Brighton, the penultimate concert in the first leg of their tour, they were exhausted, but healthy and in good spirits. They had played 26 concerts at 25 venues and once they had performed in Brighton and, finally, Bournemouth, they would have a well-earned rest. Mikey and Keith would at last get to spend a worthwhile length of time with their babies, Steve could cuddle up to his teddies at home, and Ronan and Shane could relax with their familes.

They were all looking forward to the Brighton gig. It was a good arena, with a capacity of 4,500, but the real bonus of this date was that they were booked into luxurious rooms overlooking the seafront in Brighton's best hotel, The Grand. It was some much welcomed comfort after so many long days and nights on the tour coach, snatching sleep in bunk beds. After the gig, they would have a two minute drive to the hotel, instead of a drive through the night to the next town. An added attraction to the Brighton concert was that their tour manager had organised an exclusive mid-tour party after the show for the band, their roadies and all the tour workers. The party would be held in The Grand itself, so at least the lads didn't have far to stagger once they had toasted the night with a few pints of Guinness.

The weather was unusually cold for the first day in June, so the seafront was relatively deserted for a Saturday. The sea was rough and high waves pounded the pebble beach. A chilly wind blew on to the shore, but the Boyzone fans, who had gathered early at the Brighton Centre, were oblivious of the unsettled weather. Several thousand were waiting long before the doors were due to open and their excitement brought a much needed buzz to the area. Their eager chatter and singing easily drowned out the ugly squawking from the seagulls and brightened up, what the weather had made, a dull and gloomy evening.

Now his ankle is better, Shane can enjoy the dance routines

Once inside, the girls quickly transformed a cold, silent arena into a stifling cauldron of hysteria. Nearly all the 4,500 seats were filled by the time the first support act, Deuce, came on stage. The atmosphere was incredible. The girls screamed, sang, blew whistles at an ear-piercing volume, and waved Boyzone banners. And all this was long before the five stars had even left their hotel rooms! The crazy party atmosphere continued right through the second support act, Sean Maguire. By the time he closed his act with a highly-charged version of his single, 'Good Day', the audience were going wild. As he left the stage, the tension mounted even more in anticipation of the main show.

A disc jockey played records to keep the music flowing in the arena while Boyzone made their final preparations backstage. Every tune he played was greeted with a deafening volley of high-pitched screams and whistles from fans who mistook the music for the opening of the Boyzone show. There were several false alarms during the 15-minute interval and then, suddenly, the arena was plunged into darkness. The blackness sent the screams to an even higher volume. Three white drapes hanging over the stage were raised slowly